God at Work:

Changing Lives by Teaching Law and Gospel

CONCORDIA PUBLISHING HOUSE • SAINT LOUIS

3558 S. Jefferson Ave., St. Louis, MO 63118-3968
1-800-325-3040 • www.cph.org

Readings text by Jeffrey E. Burkart, Carl Fickenscher II, David R. Maxwell, John W. Oberdeck, John T. Pless, Harold L. Senkbeil, Roger Sonnenberg, and Bryan Wolfmueller

Questions by Cynthia A. Wheeler

Editors: Thomas A. Nummela, Gail E. Pawlitz, and Cynthia A. Wheeler

Manufactured in the United States of America.

1 2 3 4 5 6 7 8 9 10 22 21 20 19 18 17 16 15 14 13

Table of Contents

So why should I care about using Law and Gospel?

Does it matter if I *know* the difference between Law and Gospel?

Does it matter *how* I teach them?

Does it matter *when* I teach them?

The answers are yes, yes, and yes again!

To find out why, note the six differences between Law and Gospel.

1. Law and Gospel differ in how they were revealed to humans.

- Everyone has the Law written in his or her heart, but not everyone has heard, understood, or believed the Gospel.
- That makes a *big difference* in how I teach.

2. Law and Gospel differ in their contents.

- The Law tells me what to do. The Gospel reveals to me what God is doing. It doesn't demand anything of me.
- I need to help my students know they sin, cannot please God, and need a Savior; and know and believe that Jesus did all the work to give us grace, mercy, salvation, and forgiveness.

3. Law and Gospel differ in their promises and how we receive them.

- The promises of the Law—eternal life and salvation—come with conditions. I must fulfill the Law perfectly. I must do the work.
- Gospel promises come without conditions. The Gospel asks nothing. Instead it offers a kind invitation, promising the grace of God, salvation, and faith. God in Christ did the work for me.
- When Law is taught without Gospel, self-righteousness or despair, anxiety, and fear reign in people's hearts.
- When Gospel is taught without the Law, sinners fall into self-justification, or think their actions don't matter, or that God doesn't care what they do. Tedium and ingratitude rule.
- I need to teach both Law and Gospel so that my students understand and trust God's grace in Christ Jesus.

4. Law and Gospel differ regarding their threats.

- Teaching the Law comes with threats. The Gospel contains no threats; rather, it decreases believers' desire to sin.
- I need to teach both messages so each can do its work.

5. **Law and Gospel differ regarding their functions and effects.**
   - Since I can't do what the Law demands, I become frustrated, discouraged, and unwilling to try. The Law shows me my sin, but it doesn't help me to get rid of it. The Law works in me and makes me contrite, but it does not comfort me. It tells me what to do but doesn't help me do it.
   - Without the Law, sin reigns and I don't realize I'm sinning.
   - While the Gospel demands faith, at same time it offers and gives me faith. It removes all terror, fear, guilt, and anguish. Instead it fills me with peace and joy in the Holy Spirit. It doesn't give me a to-do list, but it does change me into someone who cannot help but serve our Lord and others.
   - Without the Gospel, I am a lost and condemned sinner.
   - So it matters when I teach Law and Gospel because each affects my students differently.

6. **Law and Gospel differ regarding the persons to whom each teaching is to be preached.**
   - I can teach the Law to sinners who are content to be sinners.
   - I can teach the Gospel to sinners who are troubled, in need of God's grace.
   - Because each person hears the message they need to hear at that moment, I need to be able to identify and teach Law and Gospel effectively.

May the Holy Spirit inspire you and fill you with His grace and knowledge as you sharpen and improve your teaching skills!

How could I use this resource?

- Use the articles individually or in a group.
- Study one article at a time, or do a few related ones together.
- Discuss or ponder the beginning thought.
- Consider how the article impacts teaching the Christian faith.
- Talk about how the content applies to your setting.
- Use the Law and Gospel theses as a guide and summary. (See appendix on pages 78–80.)
- Read more in *Law & Gospel: How to Read and Apply the Gospel* by Carl Ferdinand Wilhelm Walther. This readers' edition also offers helpful background information.

Source for the six differences: C. F. W. Walther's first two lectures on Thesis 1. *Law and Gospel: How to Read and Apply the Bible,* pages 11–24.

Section A

Get it in your head!

What is Law and Gospel?

When we compare Holy Scripture with other writings, we notice that no book seems to be as full of contradictions as the Bible. And this seems to be true not only in minor points but also even in its main point, namely, regarding the doctrine of how we may come to God and are saved.

For instance, in one passage, the Bible offers forgiveness to all sinners, yet in another passage forgiveness of sins is withheld from all sinners. Or, in still another passage, life everlasting is offered freely to all people, but in yet another, people are directed to do something themselves in order to be saved.

This riddle can be solved when we consider that there are two entirely different doctrines in Scripture: the doctrine of the Law and the doctrine of the Gospel.

C. F. W. Walther
***Law and Gospel:** How to Read and Apply the Bible,*
introduction to lectures on Law and Gospel, page 10

A powerful paradox 1

Jeffrey E. Burkart

An opening thought [to ponder or discuss]

- Name a contradiction that you see in your everyday life.

Read this

Whenever the terms Law and Gospel are used in the same sentence, they present a powerful, and sometimes confusing, paradox—a seeming contradiction in terms.

Our theological language is full of such paradoxical duets:

- To live we must die.
- We are both righteous and sinful.
- God is hidden and revealed.
- Christians are free lords of all, subject to none, and dutiful servants of all, subject to all.

Paradoxes such as these are difficult to comprehend, especially for children who tend to want things explained in a direct fashion. Let's take a moment to define Law and Gospel so that each can be distinguished from the other, though they are inseparable (another paradox).

The Law

The Law is often defined in terms of its purposes. It keeps order and checks our behavior (a curb); it shows us our sins (a mirror); it guides us as to how to lead a God-pleasing life (a rule).

But this definition needs to be expanded if students are to realize that curbs that keep order and rules that help us do good are not the things that save us. The Law needs to be seen as that which condemns us—that which drives us to despair because of our inability to keep it.

If we say we've kept the Law, we sin because of the pride we have in our own accomplishments. When we try to keep the Law and fail, the Law drives us toward despair. We may even reject any hope of being forgiven.

The Law is a paradoxical gift; when we try to live according to its precepts, we find the gift has pretty sharp teeth. It simultaneously accuses and convicts us. Try as we might to keep it, it testifies as a witness against us.

The Gospel

The Gospel has the opposite effect. It is the proclamation of the Good News that God loves us unconditionally in Christ Jesus. In spite of all the evil that surrounds us, in spite of our transgression of His Law, God washed away our sins in the blood of His Son and brought us to faith through the power of His Spirit in our Baptism.

When we teach about the Law and Gospel, we need to make sure that children know that grace comes by faith in Jesus alone—no works we do can make us right with God.

According to repeated surveys, more than 50 percent of Lutherans believe they can do something to earn their salvation. More than half think they can keep the Law and, by keeping it, earn God's favor. Now that's a paradox that can change only through proper teaching of Law and Gospel and the power of the Holy Spirit.

God's Word so clearly shows us that these two beliefs are not true: "For by grace you have been saved through faith. And this is not your own doing; it is the gift of God, not a result of works, so that no one may boast" (Ephesians 2:8–9).

Teachers are privileged to pass on the Good News of salvation by grace through faith alone. May God bless you as you grow in God's Word, sharpen your teaching skills, and share the life-changing grace of God in Jesus our Savior.

Things to Think About (or Discuss)

- My biggest "ah-ha!" moment about this topic was . . .
- I really need to find out more about . . .
- When have I expected God to do something or give me something because I did something good for someone or for His Church?
- Where have I clearly heard and understood the Gospel, God's unconditional love for me in Christ Jesus?

Teaching the Bible with Law and Gospel eyes

2

John T. Pless

An opening thought (to ponder or discuss)

- To me, faithful teaching of the Bible means . . .

Read this

It is the great joy of Christian teachers to open God's written Word to their students. Teachers delight in introducing children to the people of the Scriptures and in sharing the narrative that begins with creation in Genesis and finishes with the eternal reign of the Lamb in the Book of Revelation.

Lutheran teachers know that in our teaching, we must read, study, instruct, and believe according to the Author's ultimate intention.

> These [things] are written so that you may believe that Jesus is the Christ, the Son of God, and that by believing you may have life in His name. (John 20:31)
>
> But as for you, continue in what you have learned and have firmly believed, knowing from whom you learned it and how from childhood you have been acquainted with the sacred writings, which are able to make you wise for salvation through faith in Christ Jesus. All Scripture is breathed out by God and profitable for teaching, for reproof, for correction, and for training in righteousness, that the man of God may be complete, equipped for every good work. (2 Timothy 3:14–17)

Teaching God's Word faithfully means teaching both Law and Gospel. One of our Lutheran Confessions, the Apology of the Augsburg Confession, puts it like this: "All Scripture ought to be distributed into these two principal topics: the Law and the promises. For in some places Scripture presents the Law, and in others the promises about Christ" (The Apology of the Augsburg Confession, Article IV, paragraph 5).

Impossible demands

Law is characterized by demand and requirement. The Apology of the Augsburg Confession reminds us that the Law, summarized in the Ten Commandments, requires not only "outward civil works, which reason can in some way produce. But they also require other things placed far above reason: truly to fear God, truly to love God, truly to call upon God, truly to be convinced that God hears us, and to expect God's aid in death and in all afflictions" (Article IV, paragraph 8). That is to say, God's Holy Law lays on us a demand that we cannot meet.

Lutheran teachers will not attempt to diminish the Law by reducing its uncompromising requirement that we fear, love, and trust in God above all things. We will recognize the Law for what it is—that good and Holy Word of God that orders our lives in this sinful world and shows us how far short we sinners fall before God.

But knowledge of the Law does not save. In fact, Satan would use the knowledge of the Law to drive your students into despair and harden them in unbelief.

Incredible love

Christ Jesus has another purpose in mind when you teach the Law according to the Scriptures. He uses the Law not to drive to desperation and false belief but to close down every path to salvation except Himself. Because Christ alone is Savior, we confess that the Law cannot save.

To use the language of our Confessions, the Law stands in the service of the promises. So teach the Law in all of its severity. Don't diminish its demands by listening to the old Adam's lies that if we do the best we can, God will do the rest. The Law requires much more than good intentions or right motivations!

The righteousness that saves is the righteousness of Jesus, who has fulfilled the Law by His sinless life, His perfect obedience, and His sin-atoning death. This is the promise that your students need to hear from you when you open the Scriptures.

Things to Think About (or Discuss)

Restate the purposes of God's Law and Gospel in your own words.

- When I am confronted with the Law, I often feel . . .
- What thoughts or fears keep me from sharing God's word of Law with my students? How can I change my thinking about this?
- What are my favorite words or images that explain the Gospel?

What is the Law? 3

John T. Pless

AN OPENING THOUGHT [TO PONDER OR DISCUSS]

- My favorite law is . . .

Read this

Reformation theologians struggled with a question that confronts teachers today who want to faithfully teach God's Law and Gospel in their classrooms. Once the Law has accused and the Gospel has created faith, what purpose does the Law serve in the Christian's life?

We see the Law at work in the world, providing order and discipline as a curb to prevent total moral chaos. The chief function of the Law, however, is as a mirror that shows us the ugliness of our sin. But do Christians need the Law? Yes, believers in Christ need the Law because we are at the same time both sinners and saints. The old Adam in us continually needs to die and drive us back to Christ Jesus for forgiveness of sins and newness of life.

Obedience to the Law does not sanctify us; Christ alone does that by His atoning death. The Law shows us what good works are, but it has no power to produce them from our sinful flesh. Only the free gift of the Gospel can create a "free, cheerful spirit" that produces the fruit of the Spirit.

The Formula of Concord carefully asserts, "When a person is born anew by God's Spirit, liberated from the Law (i.e., freed from this driver), and led by Christ's Spirit, he lives according to God's unchangeable will revealed in the Law. Since he is born anew, he does everything from a free, cheerful spirit. . . . For such people are no longer under the Law, but under grace, as St. Paul says in Romans 8:2" (Solid Declaration of the Formula of Concord, Article VI, paragraph 17).

Freedom from the Law's curse

We teach God's Law to our students to direct them away from what the Lutheran Confessions call "self-chosen works," projects we think please God but lack His commandment.

Freed from the curse of the Law, the Law remains to direct the Christian to live in the world and serve our neighbors in love. The Gospel alone rules the conscience of the Christian; the Law rules the body.

So the teacher will teach the Law in such a way that students learn to follow Luther's encouragement to embrace and claim our baptismal grace in Christ. Help students stay within set limits and practice overcoming the flesh, but don't let their consciences trouble them. Remember that we are God's beloved baptized children.

Things to Think About (or Discuss)

- What sentence popped off the page to me?
- One thing I still wonder about is . . .
- Now I understand that . . .
- How can I put these concepts to work in my teaching right away?

What is the Gospel? 4

John T. Pless

An opening thought [to ponder or discuss]

• A Gospel truth I know is . . .

Read this

Christians use the word *Gospel* frequently in our conversations and classrooms. What does this little word mean?

The Formula of Concord offers this succinct definition: "Everything that comforts, that offers God's favor and grace to transgressors of the Law, is, and is properly called, the Gospel. It is a good and joyful message that God will not punish sins, but will forgive them for Christ's sake" (Solid Declaration of the Formula of Concord, Article V, paragraph 21). In other words, the Gospel is God's own gift to comfort sinners broken by the condemnation of the Law.

God's revelation in Christ

The Gospel is never about what we do; it is always about what Christ Jesus gives us in His living, dying, and rising again from the grave.

One of Luther's favorite pictures of the Gospel was that of *testament*, the word used by Jesus when He instituted the Supper of His body and blood. We speak of the legal document that designates the distribution of a deceased person's property as "a last will and testament." The Gospel is the Lord's own last will and testament, set in motion by His death, and naming all who believe in Him as heirs of His promise and the forgiveness of sins.

The Gospel is not just good news in a bad situation. It is the Good News that God's own Son took our sin on Himself, endured a sinner's death for us, and rose again to life for those who are dead in trespasses and sin. (Explore the expanse of God's love for us in Ephesians 2:1–10.)

The Gospel declares that your students belong to Jesus. Sin, death, and the Law are not their master, because Jesus was crucified and raised to give them His own righteousness, and with it, joy and peace.

Repetition with a purpose

Sometimes we assume that our students know the Gospel, but this is both deceptive and detrimental to Christian teaching. We cannot speak the Gospel often enough. While it is necessary that the Law be taught to uncover unbelief and its varied fruits, it is only the evangelical message that God was in Christ reconciling the world to Himself that delivers the goods: forgiveness of sins, righteousness before God, peace with God, and the promise of eternal life.

> Therefore, if anyone is in Christ, he is a new creation. The old has passed away; behold, the new has come. All this is from God, who through Christ reconciled us to Himself and gave us the ministry of reconciliation; that is, in Christ God was reconciling the world to Himself, not counting their trespasses against them, and entrusting to us the message of reconciliation. Therefore, we are ambassadors for Christ, God making His appeal through us. We implore you on behalf of Christ, be reconciled to God. For our sake He made Him to be sin who knew no sin, so that in Him we might become the righteousness of God. (2 Corinthians 5:18–21)

Without Jesus' death and resurrection, there is no Gospel. And without the Gospel, there is no comfort for sinners, even young ones.

Take at look at your lessons and evaluate your words. Is the Gospel dominant—not merely assumed or alluded to—in every lesson. Make sure your teaching rings with the glad news of Jesus, Friend, and Savior of sinners. Your students need to hear it over and over again.

Our thinking and reasoning often fight against the Gospel. Because sin is at work in us all the time, we need to hear God's love, acceptance, and assurance of forgiveness again and again. May we be blessed by repetition with a purpose.

Things to think about (or discuss)

- I was surprised . . .
- I really want to find out more about . . .
- What reasons might someone give for not teaching the Gospel in every lesson?
- What does the Gospel give that we can't get anywhere else?
- Thinking back to my most recent lessons, did the Gospel dominate my words and actions? If not, what do I change?

Use every chance to teach the Gospel

5

Carl Fickenscher II

An opening thought (to ponder or discuss)

- Name a Bible story that gives challenges for teaching the Gospel.

Read this

She was nine years old, and she spent Saturday night with her friend, a student in your class. She may not have realized that Sunday School was part of the bargain. She was sleepy—she and her friend had talked long into the night after lights out—and she wasn't used to getting up on Sunday. In fact, she'd never gotten up on Sunday morning for this, never been in a Sunday School class or church in her life. Maybe she never would be again. But this day, this hour, she's in your class.

Gospel every sermon

Pastors are taught that every sermon should contain enough clear Gospel that if someone never heard a word from God before or after, that person would hear in that sermon what he or she needs to believe to be saved.

C. F. W. Walther said, "Now, [I say to] the preacher who steps out of his pulpit without having preached enough Gospel—so that some poor sinner who may have come to church for the first and the last time is not saved—woe to him! [That sinner's] blood will be required of [that preacher]!" (*Law and Gospel: How to Read and Apply the Bible,* Thesis XXV, p. 462).

We should certainly hold the same standard for every Christian education class. Of course, not every lesson is the story of Good Friday. Some weeks, in fact, it may seem as if the Bible account has nothing at all to do with Jesus' death and resurrection. We might think we accomplished the teaching task quite well by teaching the facts about Noah's ark, Paul's second missionary journey, or even Jesus teaching His disciples the Lord's Prayer.

If so, our little friend goes out the door without ever hearing that Jesus died for her sins.

Gospel in every lesson

The reality is that every Bible story is an expression of Jesus' reconciling death. Sin separated our first parents and every person since then from God. This cut us off from every good gift of God. But by taking away that separating sin, Jesus' death on the cross brought us back together with God so that we again receive His blessings. In other words, every blessing we receive—deliverance from floods, protection from angry mobs, our daily bread, forgiveness of sin—is a result of the cross.

Every story, every lesson offers opportunity to tell that one-time visitor and all of your regulars about the cross of Christ. You never know when a long-time student will grasp the truth of the Gospel as his or her own. In fact, for most Christians, this happens again and again in our lives because in the cross, we see the Gospel of our salvation.

Walther ends his series on understanding Law and Gospel with a final thesis that states that teachers should allow "the Gospel to predominate in your teaching" (Thesis XXV). How true, because the Gospel of Jesus' cross saves every one of us.

Things to Think About (or Discuss)

- This reminds me of . . .
- Now I understand that . . .
- The best opportunity that I have to hear the Gospel is . . .
- When have I grasped the truth of the Gospel as my own?
- When did I recently have a chance to share the Gospel of Christ? Did I take it? If so, what happened? If not, what stopped me?

Use the Catechism as your guide

6

John T. Pless

An opening thought (to ponder or discuss)

- When I hear the word *catechism*, I think about . . .

Read this

Teachers often overlook a vital handbook for making the distinction between Law and Gospel—Luther's Small Catechism. The catechism contains a memorable summary of Holy Scriptures; it is also a pattern to tutor us in distinguishing God's condemnation of sin from His forgiveness of sins in Christ.

Beginning with the Ten Commandments

The Law shows us our sin; the Gospel shows us the forgiveness of sins. Luther begins the catechism with the Commandments, using the Law as a mirror to reveal our failure to fear, love, and trust in God above all things.

By nature we do not want God to be our God; the whole Law is contained in the First Commandment. Sin is deeper than making mistakes or mischievous behavior. Sin clings to idols made by our own hearts. The Commandments convict us of our persistent pursuit of other idols.

But God's final Word is not the Ten Commandments. The Creed comes after the Commandments in the Catechism, just as the Gospel comes after the Law. In the Creed, we confess who the triune God is and what He has done for our salvation. If the First Commandment forbids all false idols, the Creed announces that you need no other God because you have the true God: Father, Son, and Holy Spirit.

I cannot think of a more compelling summary of the Gospel than Luther's explanation of the Second Article of the Apostles' Creed:

> I believe that Jesus Christ, true God, begotten of the Father from eternity, and also true man, born of the Virgin Mary, is my Lord, who has redeemed me, a lost

and condemned person, purchased and won me from all sins, from death, and from the power of the devil; not with gold or silver, but with His holy, precious blood and with His innocent suffering and death, that I may be His own and live under Him in His kingdom and serve Him in everlasting righteousness, innocence, and blessedness, just as He is risen from the dead, lives and reigns to all eternity. This is most certainly true.

Measure your words

As you speak the Gospel to your students, measure your words by the rule of the catechism.

- How well have you stated who Jesus is—true God, begotten of the Father from eternity, and true man, born of the Virgin Mary?
- How clearly have you stated what Jesus did for them—purchased and won us from all sins, from death, and from the power of the devil; not with gold or silver, but with His holy, precious blood and with His innocent suffering and death?
- How carefully have you clarified the outcome of Jesus' work—that I may be His own and live under Him in His kingdom and serve Him in everlasting righteousness, innocence, and blessedness?

There's more

Of course, there is much more in the catechism that will focus your teaching of the Law and Gospel.

The Lord's Prayer comes after the Creed, showing us how the certainty of who God is and what He has done forms the platform for praying with boldness and confidence. The teaching on the Sacraments makes clear how God bestows the Gospel. Daily Prayers and the Table of Duties speak to our Christian life in the world.

From beginning to end, the catechism keeps Law and Gospel clear in our teaching.

Things to Think About [or Discuss]

- I learned . . .
- I want to know more about . . .
- How do we make idols in our thinking and actions (heart)?
- An idol that my heart clings to is . . .
- How could Luther's Small Catechism help with lesson preparation or teaching?

Section B

Put some feet on it!

Teaching Law and Gospel without confusing them

My aim is to show you how easily we can inflict great damage on our hearers when we mingle Law and Gospel—despite their fundamental differences—and thus defeat the purpose of both doctrines. You cannot begin to appreciate this point until you grasp the differences between Law and Gospel.

C. F. W. Walther
Law and Gospel: *How to Read and Apply the Bible,*
Thesis I, page 11

When it comes to experience, you will find the Gospel a rare guest but the Law a constant guest in your conscience.

Martin Luther
Luther's Works,
Volume 26, page 117

7 The privilege of teaching God's Word

Roger Sonnenberg

An opening thought (to ponder or discuss)

- A privilege is . . .

Read this

A pastor recently told of his experience while living close to a large, nondenominational, metropolitan congregation. Some of the members of that large church sought him out after their lives, marriages, or families fell apart.

Although these members religiously tried to follow the strong teachings set forth by the church, they found St. Paul's words to be true: "I do not understand my own actions. For I do not do what I want, but I do the very thing I hate. . . . Who will deliver me from this body of death?" (Romans 7:15, 24).

The crushing power of the Law

The problem is simple. Churches that emphasize *behavior* as the most important sign of faith teach that the Law alone can correct flaws in a person's life. Though it has an important role, the Law does not change a person's heart. This is done only through the Gospel!

St. Paul said, "For I am not ashamed of the gospel, for it is the power of God for salvation to everyone who believes. . . . For in it the righteousness of God is revealed from faith for faith, as it is written, 'The righteous shall live by faith'" (Romans 1:16–17).

To be made *righteous* is to be made "right with God." This comes through faith in Jesus Christ, the one who lived, died, and rose so that we might have forgiveness and abundant life (John 10:10).

As forgiven people, we are not only brought into a new relationship with God; we are also given new life in Him to do on earth what we could never do on our own. We are given "the immeasurable greatness of His power toward us who believe, according to the working of His great might that He worked in Christ when He raised Him from the dead" (Ephesians 1:19–20).

The em-power-ment of the Gospel

Teaching the Law has an effect. The Law can curb sin and compel obedience. For example, many public schools today teach abstinence, which can lay out a reasonable case for waiting to have sex until marriage. Even an atheist might fear the consequences of promiscuity, such as STDs or bearing children out of wedlock, and remain celibate until marriage.

However, teaching the Law alone is not enough. Without the Gospel of Jesus Christ, we have no power other than our own with which to face this difficult task of remaining sexually pure until marriage. And while it is the Gospel that motivates good works, it is faith that makes a work good.

Many churches choose Vacation Bible School materials filled with Bible facts and platitudes about being good—the Law—but proclaim no cross, no Gospel. Kids go away knowing what they're supposed to do but not being able to do it!

Teaching about Jesus presents the privilege of sharing God's love and forgiveness. We are honored to tell others about that love. And as they hear it, the Holy Spirit moves and empowers them to be Christlike! Through the Holy Spirit working in and through us, we are given opportunity to make a difference—a true difference—in a person's life.

Things to Think About (or Discuss)

- All Law and no Gospel makes people think . . .
- I've seen too much Law at work in my life when . . .
- Do I use curriculum and resources for my classes that have a balance of Law and Gospel? If not, do I have a good enough reason to ignore this disadvantage?
- What questions do I still have about this topic?

8 The pitfalls of using the Gospel as Law

Roger Sonnenberg

An opening thought (to ponder or discuss)

- The biggest pitfall I have to watch out for in teaching is . . .

Read this

A pastor told me of overhearing a Sunday School teacher say to her student, "Clarissa, if you do that one more time, then Jesus didn't die for you." Ouch! That's one time when I truly hope the child wasn't listening to the teacher—or, if she was, that the words didn't stick.

Such words distort the biblical teaching about salvation and can mar a child's understanding of the Gospel for her entire life. The truth of the matter is that we'd all be in trouble if the teacher's words were correct. We'd be doomed to eternal death in hell on account of our repeated sinning.

Confusing Law and Gospel

This unfortunate episode forces us to think about our words and the things we say to the students entrusted to our care. Do we confuse Law and Gospel? Do we try so hard to motivate and change behavior that we turn God's Law into Gospel or His Gospel into Law?

Periodically reviewing some of the basic teachings of the Lutheran faith helps us stay on track.

Question 85 in Luther's Small Catechism with Explanation asks, "What is the difference between the Law and the Gospel?" The answer:

"A. The Law teaches what we are to do and not to do; the Gospel teaches what God has done, and still does, for our salvation.

"B. The Law shows us our sin and the wrath of God; the Gospel shows us our Savior and the grace of God.

"C. The Law must be proclaimed to all people, but especially to impenitent sinners; the Gospel must be proclaimed to sinners who are troubled in their minds because of their sins."

The words you speak

Ask yourself a few questions.

- If the children I've taught never hear any other words about Jesus, will they have heard enough from me to know the way of salvation through faith in Jesus Christ?
- Thinking about the difference between Law and Gospel, am I too heavy on Law?
- If I were a child in my classroom, would I go away frightened or joyful? Both have their place. How can I make sure children hear both messages?

Only the Gospel saves. Only the Gospel brings genuine hope, certain joy! Every Clarissa who leaves your classroom should leave knowing that despite the fact that she "did it again," Jesus loves her.

Things to Think About (or Discuss)

- Answer one or more of the questions in the reading. Discuss your response with your group or a trusted support person.
- Am I familiar with a version of Luther's Small Catechism that includes pages of questions and answers as an explanation? Most cite Scripture in the answers. How might this tool be helpful to me?
- How does God treat me when I keep "doing it again"?
- What can I do when my students keep "doing it again"?

9 A balancing act

Harold L. Senkbeil

AN OPENING THOUGHT [TO PONDER OR DISCUSS]

- Something I often mix up is . . .

Read this

The Formula of Concord says, "From the beginning of the world these two proclamations have always been taught alongside each other in God's Church with a proper *distinction*" (Solid Declaration of the Formula of Concord, Article V, paragraph 23, emphasis added).

Distinction means understanding the differences between the two proclamations and balancing their use.

Think a minute about balance.

It's not easy to keep your balance when you first start riding a bicycle. Remember all that lurching and swerving as you made your way down the driveway? No doubt you took a few tumbles before you mastered the art of defying gravity while simultaneously propelling yourself forward on two wheels. For a while it seemed like the impossible dream, didn't it? But after careful practice, you could keep up with the best of them and maybe even toss in some wheelies for good measure.

There's a balance to strive for in good teaching too. As we approach each and every text of Holy Scripture, the first thing is to determine if it is Law or Gospel. Does it command, warn, threaten, or condemn? Then you are working with God's Law. On the other hand, texts that speak of His promise, consolation, forgiveness, and salvation in Christ are clearly Gospel. So far, so good.

Teaching with balance

It gets trickier when you actually start teaching the lesson. Then you have to keep things in balance, neither confusing the Law with the Gospel nor mixing the two. It's so easy to fall off on one side or the other, either tacking conditions onto God's promises or turning His commands into consolation.

However, with careful and prayerful study, the guidance of your pastor, and much practice, you can master this art.

Two things lie at the heart of keeping Law and Gospel in proper balance—two boundaries, summarized in the sentence from the Formula of Concord at the beginning of this reading.

First, keep the Law and Gospel alongside each other; never sacrifice one at the expense of the other. It's all too easy to weasel out on the Law, shrinking away from showing how all of us sinners stand condemned and under God's judgment in our sin. Similarly, we're tempted to give short shrift to the Gospel, talking blithely about "the love of God" rather than the astounding Good News that Jesus has exchanged His righteousness for our sin.

Second, maintain the proper distinction between them; never turn one into the other. It's all too easy to turn the Law into a condition of salvation—as when so-called "Christian principles for living" become the main thrust of the message. Likewise, the Gospel is easily twisted into a message of correction and rebuke. Whenever "What would Jesus do?" obscures the preaching of the cross of Christ, sinners are robbed of the forgiveness of sins.

So, by the grace of God, keep your balance, won't you? Your students will be all the richer for it!

Things to Think About [or Discuss]

- I wonder about . . .
- What am I learning about balancing Law and Gospel?
- Say a statement that turns Law into Gospel.
- Say a statement that turns Gospel into Law.
- What can I do to avoid the pitfalls of mixing Law and Gospel?

10 More than an example

Carl Fickenscher II

AN OPENING THOUGHT (TO PONDER OR DISCUSS)

- Who is an example for me "in speech, in conduct, in love, in faith, in purity" (1 Timothy 4:12)?

Read this

When studying the Bible stories for an upcoming lesson, we should always ask the question, what's the point? What would the Holy Spirit have our children learn from this lesson?

Sometimes mistakes are made. A lesson on Solomon building the temple may lead to "You, too, can do great things for the Lord." Digging into the three men in the fiery furnace might point to "Trust God the way Shadrach, Meshach, and Abednego did." Good ideas, perhaps, but not the point.

Not what we should do

Especially with Old Testament stories, it's easy to assume that the message to be gleaned is to follow the admirable example of the biblical hero—or to avoid the sin acted out by a stumbling character.

Even with the life of Christ, though, we might trip into some common misdirections.

- Jesus prayed to His Father at the most crucial moments in His ministry, so we should likewise be diligent in prayer.
- Jesus had compassion on lepers, the blind, tax collectors, and other social outcasts, so we should be kind to the downtrodden among us also.
- Jesus was obedient even unto death because He loved us; we should be just as committed to those values that are truly important, even at great personal sacrifice.

Again, all are true, but they are not the point. C. F. W. Walther presented twenty-five theses that examine common ways the saving Gospel of Jesus Christ can be confused. He said, "The most common way people mingle Law and Gospel . . . [is] turning Christ into a kind of new Moses or Lawgiver" (*Law and Gospel: How to Read and Apply the Bible*, Thesis V).

Each of the lesson points listed even those about Jesus, offers an example—and nothing more. Jesus or an Old Testament "hero" did something; we should do something similar. Teaching that point puts the focus on us and what we are supposed do. That's pure Law. Quite simply, Law is what we are to do or not do.

Teaching Bible stories this way makes Jesus a new Lawgiver, just someone who shows us something we are to do. Law must be preached and taught, but it's never the final point.

What Jesus did

The things Jesus did—praying, having compassion, and, above all, going to the cross—were not to show us what we are to do. *Jesus' life and death were the actual doing for us of all God demands of us.* The point of each of these stories is that God in Christ Jesus does it all—obeys, trusts, loves, saves. That's the Gospel, what God in Christ has done for us.

Christ, then, is always more than just an example of one who shows us how to keep the Law. He's the one who fulfilled the Law in our place. That's Gospel—and that's the point.

Things to Think About (or Discuss)

- What is the point of this reading?
- What benefits do my students get from having examples or heroes to follow?
- What disservice do I do to the people in the Bible when I turn them into heroes to emulate? What could happen if I presented Bible people as real people who had real problems and sinned, but were forgiven by God and lived in His grace?
- What key messages do I miss teaching when I turn Jesus into someone who tells us what to do?
- What points do I really want my students to know and believe about Jesus?

11 Bootstraps and sandals

Jeffrey E. Burkart

An Opening Thought (to ponder or discuss)

- I wear my favorite pair of shoes when I . . .

Read this

Whenever we discuss the Law and the Gospel, someone in the crowd is bound to think, "Hmmm. I'm not so bad. Other people sin more than I do. God will surely look kindly on me." Children and adults can easily fall prey to this kind of thinking.

It is true that God always stands ready to bail us out of sin's prison. Jesus paid the price for our release by stepping onto the gallows and taking the fall for us. Our salvation came at a tremendous price, yet too often, we think that we deserve to be set free. We are shameless in our self-righteous attitude.

The bootstrap myth

It's fashionable to think that we can pull ourselves up by our bootstraps. Americans honor the rugged individualist in our culture, the man or woman who stands against all odds, faces danger, and triumphs in the face of adversity. We admire heroes and heroines like this. Everybody cheers Spiderman, Indiana Jones, James Bond, and Lara Croft because they beat their enemies through resourcefulness, cunning, intelligence, or strength of arm. We encourage children and young adults to "make it on their own" because "it's tough out there" in the real world.

The truth of the matter is that we are all dependent on others. Yet we buy into the myth that it's by our own "reason and strength" that we accomplish things—even our own salvation.

The servant's sandals

Whenever we think we can save ourselves from the clutches of sin by pulling on our own bootstraps, we need to look at the feet of the Master and remember that we are unworthy to carry His sandals (Matthew 3:11). To think that we can save ourselves is to miss out on the costly gift of forgiveness through the life and death of His Son. God loves us so much that He placed everyone's sins on His Son so that through Christ's death, we could be washed in the blood of the Lamb.

So, if you're looking for a true hero to save you when all is lost, look only to Jesus. He's the one and only who can save you. The only escape we have from the accusing power of the Law is the gift of faith in Christ, our Savior.

Rather than trust your ability to pull yourself out of sin by your bootstraps, humbly bear the sandals of Christ. Forgiveness is free to those who no longer look to themselves for salvation, but only to those who trust in Jesus.

Things to Think About (or Discuss)

- Name a modern hero whom you admire.
- Name someone you considered a hero who did not live up to the hype.
- Jesus was a servant when He . . .
- What does it mean to humbly bear the sandals of Christ? (Hint: see Luke 9:23–26.)

12 It's not all about me

Carl Fickenscher II

AN OPENING THOUGHT (TO PONDER OR DISCUSS)

- What Bible verse comforts me when I doubt?

Read this

If you ask your students, "How do you know you have eternal life?" you might hear responses like these:

"Because I just do. I know Jesus is going to take me to heaven."

"Because I ask Jesus to forgive my sins."

"Because I believe in Jesus."

We're probably well drilled enough to know we don't answer this question by saying "Because I've been good" or "Because I've tried to do the right things." We spot that kind of works righteousness a mile away.

But the truth is, there's a dangerous similarity between these last two obvious errors and the first three answers. Does that surprise you? Those answers are all about Jesus, about forgiveness, about faith—aren't they? Or are they really all about me?

C. F. W. Walther wrote: "You are not rightly distinguishing Law and Gospel in the Word of God if you point sinners who have been struck down and terrified by the Law toward their own prayers and struggles with God. . . . until they would feel that God has received them into grace. Rather, point them toward the Word and Sacraments" (*Law and Gospel: How to Read and Apply the Bible*, Thesis IX).

Walther called this the main, most important thesis of the twenty-five in his series. What does it mean? In capsule, Walther is saying this: our certainty of salvation is never to be found inside ourselves, but always in our Baptism, in God's Word of Gospel—especially Absolution—and in Holy Communion.

These Means of Grace (channels through which God works to give us His grace and gifts) are completely outside ourselves. They do their work without us lifting a finger, without us even lifting our hearts. And the work they do is nothing less than the giving and assuring of heaven.

That's very different from seeking assurance of salvation in what "I just know" or in the fact that "I ask Jesus" or that "I believe."

After all, there may come a time when, painfully aware of my sins, I'm not so sure I'm really saved. I may wonder if I'm really being sincere when I ask Jesus to forgive me. I may wonder if all the mixed-up feelings and doubts swimming through my head mean I don't truly believe anymore. With good intentions, we may outfit our students with such self-directed answers, but these are not the sure foundation of faith.

The foundation of faith is this: When we were baptized, Jesus gave us the forgiveness of sins and eternal life that He earned on the cross. When Pastor says "I forgive you all your sins," we are forgiven. When our students receive the body and blood of Jesus, "given and shed for you for the forgiveness of sins," they have heaven, "for where there is forgiveness of sins, there is also life and salvation" (*Luther's Small Catechism with Explanation*, Section 1, The Sacrament of the Altar). That's the answer!

"I have eternal life because the Bible says so, because I've been baptized, because Christ gives Himself to me."

Things to Think About (or Discuss)

- The biggest eye-opener for me from this reading is . . .
- How can I know that I have eternal life? Read 1 John 5:1–21. Underline every phrase that assures me of God's gift of eternal life in Christ.
- Works righteousness is the natural way people reason about situations. I do something for someone; they return the favor. Tit for tat. In what ways can this sneaky thinking creep into my teaching? How can I guard against it?

13 It's all about Jesus

John T. Pless

AN OPENING THOUGHT (TO PONDER OR DISCUSS)

- Faith is . . .

Read this

How do you speak of saving faith when you teach your students?

We confuse Law and Gospel when faith is described as a human commitment or a decision. Faith is nothing less than the gift of the Spirit bestowed by the Gospel apart from the works of the Law.

> Faith comes from hearing, and hearing through the word of Christ. (Romans 10:17)
>
> For by grace you have been saved through faith. And this is not your own doing; it is the gift of God, not a result of works, so that no one may boast. (Ephesians 2:8–9)

The clarity of the Gospel is dulled when a description of faith focuses on its characteristics or qualities rather than on its object and content: Christ Jesus and His gift of forgiveness of sins.

This leads people to think in terms of measurements: Is my faith strong enough? Do I really have faith? Faith becomes the ultimate good work that the believer must somehow accomplish. Trust in my faith replaces trust in Christ alone.

Faith is not our work

C. F. W. Walther pinpoints a particularly subtle way of confusing the Law with the Gospel when he wrote, "You are not rightly distinguishing Law and Gospel in the Word of God if you explain faith by demanding that people are able to make themselves believe or at least can collaborate toward that end. Rather, preach faith into people's hearts by laying the Gospel promises before them" (*Law and Gospel: How to Read and Apply the Bible*, Thesis XIII).

Walther cautions teachers to use careful descriptions of faith. For example, in teaching a lesson on the fruit of the Spirit listed in Galatians 5:22–23, a teacher should avoid statements such as "A true Christian is always loving, joyful, peaceful, patient, kind, good, faithful, gentle, and self-controlled."

To be sure, the Holy Spirit working through God's Word and Sacraments produces these virtues in Christians. But does such a statement honestly fit all believers at all times?

Hardly! There are times when genuine believers are anything but joyful, peaceful, patient, and so forth. A person who is quick-tempered, sullen, or anxious does not automatically lose these traits once he or she becomes a Christian. Christians, like unbelievers, possess a variety of personality traits and dispositions.

To be sure, faith produces fruit in works of love, but the works are not to be confused with faith itself. Faith is not a work we do; it is trust in Jesus Christ's work for us.

Faith trusts Jesus

So the best way to talk about faith is to talk about Jesus and what He has done for us, both in His life of active obedience to His Father's will and in His passive suffering and death for sinners.

Any talk about faith that is not talk about Jesus' saving work for us muddles the Law with the Gospel, inviting uncertainty and ultimately leading to either despair or self-righteousness.

Faith is known not by the varying virtues of believers but by its content, Christ Jesus. He is a one-size-fits-all Savior, for His righteousness is completely sufficient for all sinners at all times.

Things to Think About (or Discuss)

- What kinds of things do people trust in the world? (What idols do they worship?)
- What phrases wrongly describe faith as something we do?
- How is faith in Jesus different than trust shown in the world?
- How should Christians deal with each other when we fail or hurt each other?
- How is Jesus' righteousness sufficient for all sinners at all times?

14 The Gospel is always a surprise

Bryan Wolfmueller

AN OPENING THOUGHT (TO PONDER OR DISCUSS)

- I was recently surprised by . . .

Read this

We love surprises.

When you think you've performed poorly on a test, you are surprised and delighted to see an A written on the top of the page.

When you are sick, you rejoice to hear unexpected news that your test results are normal.

When a loved one returns early from a business trip or brings you an extravagant gift for no reason at all, it makes your day.

These are all wonderful surprises, but the greatest surprise is the Gospel.

Christians are very familiar with the Gospel. We hear of Jesus' death on the cross bringing us the forgiveness of all our sins in sermons, throughout the Divine Service, and coming out of our own mouths as we teach our students. This is wonderful! The more Gospel, the better. However, with this familiarity there comes a peculiar danger. It may be that the Gospel can lose its joy and delight—its surprise!

What we expect

The Gospel is robbed of its wonder when the teaching of the Law does not precede it.

After all, what should we expect from God? What do we deserve from Him? His grace? No! God's Law reveals to us that we are sinners. In thought, word, and deed, we have offended God. When we consider our own lives, we see exactly who we are—sinners, ungodly and unholy. What we deserve from God is His wrath, anger, and condemnation. We deserve to be rejected.

When we know this, the Gospel surprises us. Instead of wrath, we get God's good pleasure! Where we should see His anger, we see His smile. Instead of condemnation, eternal life. Instead of hearing "Depart from me, you wicked servant," we hear "Well done, good and faithful servant, welcome to the joy of your Master."

All of this is a pure gift, pure grace and mercy, the surprise of the Gospel. This is totally undeserved. That's real Gospel! What a surprise!

What we hear

God speaks kindly to us sinners, "Your sins are all forgiven," and we are surprised. "Me! My sins! Do You know what I've done?" "Yes," says our Lord Jesus. "Your sins. Every one of them is died for, covered with My blood, forgiven. My death was for you." "For me? All for me?" "Yes. All for you!" This is the surprise of the Gospel.

When the Law and the Gospel are in their proper place, the Gospel will always be a wonderful, unexpected, delightful surprise. Make no mistake: this surprise is exactly what the Lord planned.

Things to Think About (or Discuss)

- The most surprising thing to me in this reading was . . .
- Why is the Gospel surprising?
- When was the last time I was surprised by the Gospel? If I haven't been surprised lately, what might I need?
- Why do the Law and the Gospel need to be preached and taught together?
- How does a partial statement such as "God loves you" rob people of the joy of the Gospel? What else is needed?

15 A brilliant light

Harold L. Senkbeil

An opening thought (to ponder or discuss)

- The brightest light I've ever seen was . . .

Read this

> The distinction between the Law and the Gospel is a particularly brilliant light. It serves the purpose of rightly dividing God's Word (2 Tim. 2:15) and properly explaining and understanding the Scriptures of the holy prophets and apostles. We must guard this distinction with special care, so that these two doctrines may not be mixed with each other, or a law be made out of the Gospel.
>
> Solid Declaration of the Formula of Concord
> Article V, paragraph 1

Do you know what happens when you confuse baking soda with sugar when whipping up one of your favorite desserts? It might look all right, but nobody can eat it!

The pitfalls of the kitchen spill over into the classroom when we confuse the Law with the Gospel. When we mix the two, we end up with a mess.

The Law of God includes all His commands and threats; the Gospel consists of His promises and gifts in Christ. But it's so easy to confuse them. That's exactly what happens when we talk about the promises of God as if they were commands or describe the commands of God as though they were promises.

For example, when a child is deliberately bothering a classmate, you might be tempted to say, "Jesus doesn't love you when you do that." Or maybe, "Did you know that Jesus loves people who are nice to other people?"

But think about that for a minute: Does the love of Christ depend on our obedience to God's Law? Or does it flow freely from His sacrificial death for us on His cross? Indeed, this child needs to be brought to sorrow over mean-spirited actions, but the right tool to bring about repentance is not the Gospel, but the Law: "God warns us not to hurt or harm our neighbor."

When the child expresses remorse or sorrow over what was done, then you (and the child who was bothered) have the joyful privilege of forgiving the sinner: "Jesus loves and forgives you, and I do too!"

The quotation at the beginning comes from the Formula of Concord, one of our Lutheran Confessions, books that summarize what our Church teaches on the basis of the Bible. This "brilliant light" is a helpful guide as we take on the challenging and joyful task of properly applying Law and Gospel in our teaching.

Things to Think About (or discuss)

- Now I understand that . . .
- Have I ever read the Lutheran Confessions? If so, which one? If not, has my interest been piqued?
- How can I use the Law to correct behavior and bring about repentance in the classroom?
- Is it right to withhold forgiveness until a sinner repents?
- Is it right to withhold forgiveness of sin when a sinner repents?

SECTION C

Put flesh on it!

Connecting our teaching to worship and the Sacraments

According to the Holy Scriptures, Baptism is not a mere washing with earthly water. Rather, the Spirit of God—or, more precisely, Jesus, with His blood—connects with it in order to cleanse people of their sins.

Therefore, Ananias says to Saul, "Rise and be baptized and wash away your sins" (Acts 22:16), and Jesus says to Nicodemus, "Truly, truly, I say to you, unless one is born of water and the Spirit, he cannot enter the kingdom of God" (John 3:5). He mentions the water first, and then the Spirit, for it is by this very baptizing with water that the Spirit is to be given to us. . . .

According to the Holy Scriptures, the Lord's Supper is not an earthly feast but a heavenly feast on earth, in which bread and wine, the body and blood of Christ, and also forgiveness of sins, life, and salvation are given to us and sealed for us.

C. F. W. Walther
Law and Gospel: *How to Read and Apply the Bible,*
Thesis IX, page 168

Law and Gospel in worship 16

Harold L. Senkbeil

AN OPENING THOUGHT [TO PONDER OR DISCUSS]

- The best sermon I heard lately was about . . .

Read this

Bring up the topic of worship, and you may be in for a long discussion. Tensions run high between advocates of contemporary and liturgical worship and the effectiveness of each for mission in our turbulent times.

Two essentials must be kept clearly in mind:

- First, worship is for the believing baptized, not those who cannot confess that Jesus Christ is Lord.
- Second, worship never involves merely personal likes and dislikes; rather, it's a matter of faithfulness to the Gospel itself.

At the heart of the Church's life is the Gospel from which she derives her entire life and mission. The Good News is that "in Christ God was reconciling the world to Himself, not counting their trespasses against them" (2 Corinthians 5:19). It is not a product we are selling to potential customers, but "the gospel . . . [which] is the power of God for salvation to everyone who believes" (Romans 1:16).

Faith is that worship which receives the benefits that God offers; the righteousness of the Law is that worship which offers God our own merits. "God wants to be worshiped through faith so that we receive from Him those things He promises and offers" (Apology of the Augsburg Confession, Article IV, paragraph 49).

There's a Law/Gospel framework for worship, just as there is for teaching and preaching. Worship is not what we do for Him (Law), but what He does for us (Gospel). We're not trying to make God "smile" by what we do in worship; His magnificent smile already beams clearly on all the sinners in the entire world.

God's smile is hidden under the degradation of the cross, where His sinless Son took our sin and gave us His righteousness. "For our sake He made Him to be sin who knew no sin, so that in Him we might become the righteousness of God" (2 Corinthians 5:21).

Lutheran Christians have a wonderfully clear grip on the centrality of this Gospel and its sole content: Jesus Christ and Him crucified. "We preach Christ crucified, a stumbling block to Jews and folly to Gentiles" (1 Corinthians 1:23). It's our privilege to pass this treasure on to each generation in succession.

So when you teach the children in your class to worship, help them see its heart and center. Show them that worship is not about me—the songs I like to sing and things I like to hear. I bring nothing to God except my sin. Real worship centers on Jesus and the gifts He brings us: the forgiveness of sins, life, and salvation.

In every worship service, our heavenly Father gives us these gifts through His Son, in the power of His Spirit, by means of the Gospel preached and the Sacraments administered.

We are privileged to gather as God's people wherever His Word and Sacraments are, for there He has promised to be present with His gifts. Worship that honors God is pure Gospel: receiving His magnificent gifts empty-handed, by faith alone.

Things to Think About (or Discuss)

- Worship is . . .
- How does the idea that God gives His gifts to us in worship, rather than us giving things to Him, challenge my thinking about worship?
- What do I bring to worship? What do I get? What would I tell someone who said they didn't need to go to church?
- How can I help my students understand the importance of worship?

Does it matter which church you attend? 17

Carl Fickenscher II

An opening thought [to ponder or discuss]

- What do I think: are people Christians if they do not believe the same things we do?

Read this

Every student in your class has connections to other denominations: a close friend who is active in another church's youth ministry, a grandma who faithfully attends a Baptist church, or cousins who belong to a different Lutheran synod. So, what do you do if, as you're teaching about Jesus instituting His Supper, a lively conversation about other denominations picks up?

- "My grandma said it's just kinda like Jesus' body and blood."
- "How come they won't let my cousins go to Communion here?"
- "My friend already goes to Communion at her church."

It's about people

We always need to be sensitive when talking about other beliefs and denominations, because our students, like their parents and all the rest of us, always think about people, not about beliefs and denominations. We ask, "Will Grandma still go to heaven?" not "Are Baptists going to heaven?"

C. F. W. Walther makes an important distinction in his twentieth thesis about Law and Gospel. He writes that it's a confusion of Law and Gospel when a person is thought to be lost because he or she doesn't belong to the "visible orthodox Church" (that is, the church that teaches the Scriptures correctly in all points) or to those "erring in any article of faith."

A person who belongs to a church that teaches incorrectly on some points, or even holds to some errors, may still go to heaven. The Lutheran Church has consistently taught that there are true believers in Jesus in other church bodies and that everyone who believes that Jesus' death and resurrection has saved him or her does indeed have eternal life.

It's about belief

Still, we ought not suggest to our students that it makes no difference which church, Bible study, or Christian education program someone attends. Since the Holy Spirit uses the Word and Sacraments, the Means of Grace, to keep us believing in Jesus (a necessity for salvation), we want to be in the church body where that Word is rightly taught and the Sacraments are used properly.

Walther is careful not to speak condemningly of those Christians (see Preface to the Christian Book of Concord 20). There are people, like Grandma, who believe in Jesus but don't understand the real presence of Christ in Holy Communion. But Walther is firm in warning against the false teachings of erring denominations, because false teachings prevent dear souls from hearing some of the truths and receiving the gifts that the Holy Spirit uses to keep their faith in Jesus strong.

Caring for our students means we clearly and gently make that same distinction. Let's teach them to choose the church body that proclaims Christ in all Scripture's fullness. It matters! And we'll assure them that all Christ's people, all those who trust in Him, will share with us in His eternal blessings.

Things to Think About (or Discuss)

- This reminds me . . .
- How can I teach my students to choose a church based on its teaching instead of services and programs it offers?
- So, where do I draw the line? Are those who reject the Trinity considered Christians? For example, although Mormons talk about the Father, Son, and Holy Spirit, they reject the teaching of the Trinity. They consider the Father, Son, and Holy Spirit separate gods, and believe in the existence of others too. Are they Christians? Could there be Christians among the Mormons, people who put their faith in Christ crucified?
- What would I say to someone who was concerned for the salvation of a loved one who attended a different denomination?

Sacraments speak the Gospel 18

John T. Pless

An opening thought (to ponder or discuss)

- One question I have about Baptism or Holy Communion is . . .

Read this

How do you speak about Holy Baptism and the Lord's Supper to your students? Far from being addenda to the Gospel, the Sacraments are God's Means of Grace, a channel that delivers His grace to us.

The Sacraments are gifts of the Gospel, not works of the Law. They bestow Christ's blessings, not based on our performance but by His promise, a promise received through faith alone.

God's work, not ours

C. F. W. Walther said that Law and the Gospel are confused "if you teach that the Sacraments save *ex opere operata*, that is, merely by their outward performance" (*Law and Gospel: How to Read and Apply the Bible*, Thesis XXI).

In other words, the Sacraments work because God promises to bless us through them, not because we engage in the ritual of washing or of eating and drinking.

Teachers will be careful, therefore, to teach their students that Baptism is not a legalistic requirement in addition to faith. The same could be said for the Lord's Supper.

Baptism is the washing from sin that the triune God gives as He connects His Word with the water.

Teachers must consistently point out that the Lord's Supper is not a meal that we share to remember Jesus or give Him our thanks. In the Lord's Supper, Jesus Himself is the Host who gives us His body and blood to eat and to drink under the bread and the wine. It is His testament; we are His heirs to whom He gives forgiveness of sins.

Faith does not make the Sacraments, but through faith we receive the benefits promised in Baptism and the Lord's Supper.

Cling to the promise

To teach the Sacraments rightly, the Law must be distinguished from the Gospel. Teachers would do well to review both the Small and the Large Catechisms to focus their teaching of Baptism and the Lord's Supper. Especially note how Luther moves in the Small Catechism from a basic definition of Baptism and the Sacrament of the Altar to the foundation in the words of Jesus, to the benefits we receive, and finally, to the right use of the Sacraments, distinguishing the Gospel from the Law.

We want our students to cling in faith to the promises the triune God has made them in Holy Baptism. We want them to come to eat and drink Christ's body and blood, firmly trusting in the forgiveness of sins won on Calvary and now distributed in Jesus' last will and testament. Where the Law and the Gospel are rightly distinguished, students will rejoice in the bounty of Jesus' gifts bestowed in Holy Baptism and the Sacrament of the Altar, received through faith alone.

Things to Think About (or Discuss)

- I learned . . .
- I want to learn more about . . .
- Through faith alone we receive . . .
- How can I put this information to use in my class right away?

Section
D

Get to the heart!

The Law and Gospel at work in your class

When Peter preached the Law to his hearers at Pentecost, we are told [that] "they were cut to their heart." They asked him and the rest of the apostles: "Brothers, what shall we do" in order to be saved? Then Peter said to them: "Repent and be baptized every one of you in the name of Jesus Christ for the forgiveness of your sins, and you will receive the gift of the Holy Spirit" (Acts 2:38).

The effects of the Gospel are of an entirely different nature. In the first place, while the Gospel demands faith, at the same time it also offers and gives us faith. When we preach to people: "Believe in the Lord Jesus Christ!" God gives them faith through our preaching. We preach faith and any person not willfully resisting obtains faith. It is indeed not the mere physical sound of the spoken Word that produces this effect, but rather the contents of the Word.

The second effect of the Gospel is that it does not rebuke sinners at all, but rather takes all terror, all fear, all anguish from them, filling them with peace and joy in the Holy Spirit....

In the third place, the Gospel does not require people to furnish anything good—neither a good heart nor a good disposition nor an improvement of their condition, neither piousness nor love—whether toward God or men. The gospel issues no orders. Rather, it changes people. It plants love into their heart and makes them capable of all good works. It demands nothing, but gives all. Should not this fact make us leap for joy?

C. F. W. Walther
Law and Gospel: *How to Read and Apply the Bible,*
Thesis I, page 20

19 The danger of comparing students

Carl Fickenscher II

AN OPENING THOUGHT (TO PONDER OR DISCUSS)

- One value of comparing things is . . .

Read this

You have well-behaved students in your class. You also have some who do not always behave. Are you ever tempted to draw attention to the good students as role models for others?

"Why can't all of you be more like Emma?"

Be cautious! Don't paint good students as more faithful or better Christians than others.

This is a danger C. F. W. Walther anticipated: "You are not rightly distinguishing Law and Gospel in the Word of God if you describe believers in a way that is not always realistic—both with regard to the strength of their faith and to the feeling and fruitfulness of their faith" (*Law and Gospel: How to Read and Apply the Bible*, Thesis XVII).

In other words, we shouldn't describe believers in ways that do not fit all believers at all times.

Walther offers several examples. A preacher might suggest that believers are "as patient as Job," that they are always fervent in prayer, that they never fall into certain especially ugly sins, or that they don't fear death.

Hooey! Most true Christians get impatient (as Job did). They sometimes give prayer time short shrift. And Christians frequently behave in very unchristian ways. They're not usually crazy about dying. They're still Christians. They still believe in Jesus as Savior. They are still on their way to heaven—despite their highly imperfect faith.

Imagine the impact, though, of hearing that real Christian faith never stumbles or wavers. The only reasonable conclusion for almost all of us to reach must be that "I'm not a Christian after all."

Real Christian students talk out of turn—some quite often. Real believing children of God have minds that wander and attention spans that are short. Young people of real faith miss the point of your skillful teaching.

There are others who know more answers, find the Bible passages more quickly, and sit quietly. But they are not more Christian. They, too, are sinners who have been redeemed by the blood of Christ. They, too, will often waiver in faith. They may even feel a bit uneasy when held up as a good example to others, fearing quite rightly that they themselves might fall off the pedestal at any moment.

Compliments for exceptional performance are certainly in order. Walther even observes that you might even point to the actions of strong or exceptionally faithful Christians as encouraging examples to all. But such examples are never to set the bar, set the standard, for everyone else. Christ met the standard for everyone.

Things to Think About (or Discuss)

- How do I feel when people compare me with others? What feelings surface if I'm the "good one"? the "bad one"? How are both equally dangerous to the Christian faith?
- What dangers do I encounter when I hold someone up as an example or hero?
- What's the difference between comparing students and pointing someone out as an encouraging example?
- What needs to change in my thinking in order to put these concepts to work in my teaching?

20 Teaching repentance

John T. Pless

AN OPENING THOUGHT (TO PONDER OR DISCUSS)

- *Repent* means . . .

Read this

The risen Lord Jesus commissioned His disciples to proclaim repentance and faith in His name to the nations (Luke 24:47). Repentance is critical to our faith, but we can get confused notions about it when the Law and the Gospel are confused.

The word *repentance* is used in the narrow sense to signify the knowledge of sin, as when Jesus said, "The time is fulfilled, and the kingdom of God is at hand; repent and believe in the gospel" (Mark 1:15); and when Paul described his ministry of "testifying both to Jews and to Greeks of repentance toward God and of faith in our Lord Jesus Christ" (Acts 20:21).

Repentance is used in a wide sense to embrace both knowledge of sin and faith as Peter preached at Pentecost: "Repent and be baptized every one of you in the name of Jesus Christ for the forgiveness of your sins, and you will receive the gift of the Holy Spirit" (Acts 2:38).

C. F. W. Walther noted that we do not rightly distinguish Law and Gospel in the Word of God "if [we] turn the Gospel into a preaching of repentance" (Thesis XV) or when faith is preached before repentance (Thesis VII). Christian teachers should be clear about what repentance is and how it relates to saving faith.

The role of the Law

The Law is taught to work repentance, that is, to crush every effort of our sinful nature to establish our own righteousness before God. This teaching is not good news; it is unable to create the right relationship with God that it demands. Instead, it convicts us of the failure to fear, love, and trust in God above all things. It shows that the end of such unbelief is only death and condemnation.

We teach the Law so that our students may know their sin and the futility of every attempt to establish their own identity before God on the basis of human performance. The teaching of repentance tutors students in dying to sin. This is the work of the Law, not the Gospel.

The role of the Gospel

The Gospel does not teach us how to do something, not even how to repent. The Gospel announces and bestows what Christ our Righteousness has done for us.

According to the Formula of Concord, "The Law and the Gospel are also contrasted with each other. . . . We believe, teach, and confess that the Gospel is not a preaching of repentance or rebuke. But it is properly nothing other than a preaching of consolation and a joyful message that does not rebuke or terrify. The Gospel comforts consciences against the terrors of the Law, points only to Christ's merit, and raises them up again by the lovely preaching of God's grace and favor, gained through Christ's merit" (Epitome of the Formula of Concord, Article V, paragraph 7).

Christian teachers must not make Christ into a new Moses, that is, equate teaching against sin with teaching the Gospel. Rather, we teach Moses (the Law) so that our students might see sin as no light thing but the unbelief that separates from God in thought, word, and deed.

The Law works repentance, but it is the Gospel alone that proclaims God's unmitigated favor toward us in Christ Jesus. It is that Good News alone that has the power to save and enliven us for good works that are pleasing to God and useful for the neighbor.

Things to Think About (or Discuss)

- Ah-ha! So this means that . . .
- I'm still confused about . . .
- Jesus said, "Repent and believe in the gospel" (Mark 1:15). Which part of His words are Law? Where is the Gospel message?
- How can I start using this information right now?

21 Getting your students to believe (is not your job)

John T. Pless

An opening thought (to ponder or discuss)

- Faith in Christ our Savior is . . .

Read this

Christian teachers want our students to trust in Jesus Christ, to trust God's Word for the forgiveness of their sins, to live lives of faith now, and to enter God's heavenly kingdom when they die. But how do we teach faith?

In answering this question, we are challenged to distinguish between God's Law and Gospel. C. F. W. Walther said it like this:

> "You are not rightly distinguishing Law and Gospel in the Word of God if you explain faith by demanding that people are able to make themselves believe or at least can collaborate toward that end. Rather, preach faith into people's hearts by laying the Gospel promises before them" (*Law and Gospel: How to Read and Apply the Bible,* Thesis XIII).

Faith comes through the Gospel

God's Law demands faith, but it is only the Gospel that gives faith.

Law and Gospel are muddled when we think we can cause someone to come to faith by cajoling them to believe. Our exhortations and urgings cannot create faith. Only the Good News that Jesus is a Savior who is for them in life and in death can do that job. "Faith comes from hearing, and hearing through the word of Christ" (Romans 10:17).

Likewise, the Scriptures are realistic about our human condition. Apart from Jesus, "you were dead in trespasses and sins" (Ephesians 2:1).

Corpses can never will themselves to life. If the dead come back to life, they must be made alive; they cannot resuscitate themselves. The Holy Spirit breathes the breath of life into us through the Gospel.

The meaning of the Third Article of the Apostles Creed in the Small Catechism expresses it with wonderful clarity: "I believe that I cannot by my own reason or strength believe in Jesus Christ, my Lord, or come to Him; but the Holy Spirit has called me by the Gospel, enlightened me with His gifts, sanctified and kept me in the true faith."

Faith is a gift of God

Faith is not a decision or a commitment that the teacher can evoke from a student. It is a gift that God bestows through the speaking of the Good News about Jesus.

God uses teachers as instruments to speak the promises of God into the ears of their students. It is vital that you do this job because through those precious promises, He creates faith in the hearts of those who hear the Gospel. This work of the Spirit happens when and where it pleases Him.

This is a real relief and comfort for Christian teachers! God spares us the burden of attempting to make our students believe. Our calling is simply to teach faithfully the promises of God given to us in His Scriptures with truthfulness and clarity.

Where His Word is taught, God Himself creates faith. That task is in His hands, not yours. That is good news for teachers and students alike.

Things to Think About (or Discuss)

- My job as a Christian teacher is to . . .
- In light of this reading, when I think about my responsibility as a teacher, I . . .
- The work of the Holy Spirit includes . . .
- What is my favorite promise of God in the Bible right now?

22 Dealing with feelings

John T. Pless

AN OPENING THOUGHT (TO PONDER OR DISCUSS)

- Today, I feel . . .

Read this

C. F. W. Walther offered sage counsel applicable to teachers when he wrote, "Do not forget that the blessedness of Christians is not based on pleasant feelings but on the assurance that, despite the bitterest feelings imaginable, Christians are accepted by God. In their dying hour they will be received into heaven" (*Law and Gospel: How to Read and Apply the Bible,* Thesis XVII, p. 347).

Wise teachers will be careful not to describe the Christian life in such a way that equates saving faith with a mental attitude, feelings, or the absence of particular traits.

Personality quirks

In our age, where many eagerly measure spiritual progress on the basis of outward signs of personal transformation, Lutheran teachers work with a more realistic understanding of human nature. He or she recognizes that the forgiveness of sins gives us a righteousness outside ourselves—the righteousness acquired for us by the blood of Jesus Christ. However, it does not give us a new personality.

Walther wrote:

> Furthermore, you must keep in mind that Christians retain their natural temperament even after their conversion. A person with an irritable temper will keep that tendency, and it may frequently get the better of him.
>
> So do not say that, when a person becomes a Christian, he turns from a bear into a lamb, in the sense that he is willing to take rebukes and scorn from everybody and will always be ready to forgive others.

> No, [some] Christians often have great trouble keeping their temper. Frequently they cannot control it, and nobody can calm them down. Their nasty temperament will always get the upper hand. Yet we must not think that if that person were to die tonight, he would go to hell. (*Law and Gospel: How to Read and Apply the Bible,* Thesis XVII, p. 348)

Cleansed by the Gospel

Law and Gospel are confused if a teacher draws a false picture of Christians as possessors of a particular character. We can't say that a Christian is always joyful, patient, unafraid of death, and ready to forgive.

Our students are saints and sinners at the same time. Teaching shaped by this truth uses both God's Law and His Gospel. The Law is used not to change character or urge a new attitude; instead, it is a divine mirror to show our old Adam in all of his ugliness as an enemy of God. God's Law is the wrecking ball that demolishes all that is not in Christ, but it is powerless to build the new man.

The Holy Spirit builds the new man by the Gospel alone, the Good News that God's Son lived a perfect life of obedience in our place and offered His sinless life as a sacrifice for our sin.

Christian teaching is not about attitude adjustment, behavior modification, or the manipulation of emotions. It is about telling the Good News of Jesus, whose blood cleanses us from all sin, frees us from dead works, and gives us a new mind made alive by His Spirit.

Things to Think About (or Discuss)

- About this reading, I feel . . .
- If I judge my faith based on my feelings . . .
- Name Christians I know who do not always meet the standard of our Christian virtues of love, patience, kindness, and the like. What comfort does God offer to these sinners?
- How can I put this reading to work in my class? What do I need to change?

23 Changing hearts and behaviors

Carl Fickenscher II

An opening thought (to ponder or discuss)

- Discipline is . . .

Read this

Let's face it. He's not the easiest child to have in class. And it's not just a matter of his talking out of turn and not staying in his seat. It's what he sometimes says, and what he often does. It's clear he's not learning anything, and he distracts the other students. Sometimes they follow his lead. They're not learning either.

Oh, what you'd give to have him be quiet and cooperative! How much more pleasant for you and everyone else in the class! How much better for him!

Maybe. Maybe not. Frankly, it depends on what's happened inside him. And that may be determined by how you go about "changing him."

Changing behavior

C. F. W. Walther said it this way: "You are not rightly distinguishing Law and Gospel in the Word of God if you claim that people are truly converted when they get rid of certain vices and, instead, engage in certain works of piety and virtuous practices" (*Law and Gospel: How to Read and Apply the Bible*, Thesis XVI).

Essentially, Walther said that just getting someone to clean up outward behavior is no grand accomplishment. The unbelieving abuser of alcohol who simply stops drinking is still on his way to hell. The promiscuous woman who doesn't know Christ may be scared enough of AIDS to abstain, but she is no safer eternally. The boy who now sits in his seat out of guilt or fear may not be any better off than when he ran wild.

Sure, a harmonious classroom is more pleasant and more conducive to learning. You want that, and you'll be creative in trying to foster it.

But your goal as a teacher—and in every interaction you as a Christian have with others—is to change not outward behavior but hearts.

Changing hearts

You can change behavior with rules, discipline, and, perhaps, punishment—even by making students feel guilty about disappointing Jesus. In theological terms, we call that the first use of the Law—pure coercion.

Hearts, on the other hand, are only changed for the better by the Gospel, the Good News of what God has done for us in Christ. Jesus showed His love for us by dying for us on the cross. God offers forgiveness for Jesus' sake for disorderly conduct and more. The invitation to dump on Jesus' shoulders whatever it is that's really bothering us—that's what changes us inside.

It's not easy. And, if you settle for an orderly classroom, the Law may get quicker results. But you're in it for the long term, the eternal term, for salvation. The Law has its God-ordained role, but salvation comes by the Gospel.

Things to Think About (or discuss)

- Wow! This blew me away: . . .
- Regarding classroom discipline, I think . . .
- The Law motivates short-term change. The Gospel brings salvation, making a new person in Christ. God's love in Christ motivates Christians and gives them long-term, eternal change. How can I use these truths with my class?
- What are some long-term, Gospel-centered strategies that I can use in my class?

24 Teachable moments

Carl Fickenscher II

AN OPENING THOUGHT (TO PONDER OR DISCUSS)

- A moment that sticks out in my mind from my experiences with Christian education classes is . . .

Read this

There is a vital question we can ask in every interaction Christians have with other people: Is this a Law moment or a Gospel moment?

What's the question?

Every time a parishioner comes to see the pastor, every time a Christian education teacher looks out at the young souls in her or his charge, every time a believer in Christ greets a friend at the grocery store, the question is, what word from God does my member (student, friend) need to hear right now?

Does he or she need to hear that because of some sin not repented, because of reliance on self, all is not well with his or her relationship with God at this moment? Or does this same dear person need to hear instead that all sin is forgiven and that God is near and will never forsake us because Christ Jesus on the cross reconciled all people to Him? Is it a Law moment or a Gospel moment?

This is the question C. F. W. Walther suggested we must raise and answer. Walther said, "If you wish to be an orthodox teacher, you must present all the articles of faith in accordance with Scripture, yet [you] must also rightly **distinguish** Law and Gospel" (*Law and Gospel: How to Read and Apply the Bible*, Thesis II).

This is also what St. Paul meant when he said that faithful teaching is "rightly handling the word of truth" (2 Timothy 2:15).

Law or Gospel?

The "word of truth" is all of Holy Scripture, but God speaks in Scripture in two ways. In countless passages, He tells us of our sin, our helplessness, our need for a Savior; that's Law. In all the rest of the Bible, He assures us that we have forgiveness, that we have been saved and are being given all we need in Christ Jesus; that's Gospel.

God speaks to us in these two different ways because at one moment, we need to hear one, and at another moment, we need to hear the other. Rightly handling the word means giving every person we meet the Word they need right now.

A Law moment, a moment when another soul needs to hear Law, looks like Cain staring down God and denying he knew anything about Abel's murder—or like a world blatantly ignoring God's warnings in the days of Noah.

A Law moment looks like a classroom in which side conversations about blush and eyeliner or skateboarding and iPods drown out the teacher's words about God's grace in His Son.

A Gospel moment—which may come just seconds later, immediately after the Law does its work—looks like Cain, desperate because his punishment is more than he can bear, or like heads hung in shame because they've been so disrespectful.

A Law moment sounds like "I don't care" or "So what?"

A Gospel moment sounds like "I'm sorry" or "What can I do now?"

The faithful teacher—or pastor or friend—gives the Word from God that the moment demands.

Things to Think About [or discuss]

- Is a teachable moment Law? Gospel?
- Think about a time when Jesus used a teachable moment. Tell your group about it or share it with a Christian friend this week.
- At a moment's notice, a teacher might be called on to use the Law or the Gospel. Which do I feel more comfortable speaking? Practice speaking both messages as if you were with your students.
- I learned . . .

25 No excuses!

John W. Oberdeck

An opening thought (to ponder or discuss)

- What's my favorite excuse?

Read this

I'm sorry. It's all my fault. I made a mistake. I shouldn't have done that. Please forgive me.

If these words of confession and apology are difficult for mature, Christian adults—even teachers and pastors—to say, how much more difficult must they be for your students, especially if you teach children or youth?

How do we teach confession in light of Law and Gospel in our Christian education classes and in our lives?

God's Law, imperfectly written in our consciences since the fall of Adam and perfectly written in the Bible by the apostles and prophets, always accuses us. God's Law accurately details our faults and spotlights our errors. No matter how much we might deny or ignore our sins, we cannot disprove or deny the Law's painfully accurate description of our sins.

Yeah, but

So we often try to excuse our sins instead. Such an excuse is plainly evident as soon as it is spoken. Teachers hear it often.

"Yeah, but" confesses child who has been nabbed by the Law:

- "I wrote with marker on Jackie's paper, but she was making faces at me."
- "I hit him," the boy with a cut lip says as he's dragged away from his kicking enemy on the playground, "but he started it."

As soon as the sin is revealed, finger pointing begins. So common is this shifting of blame in the classroom that teachers are surprised when it doesn't happen!

We understand why the excuses happen; we use them ourselves. Shifting the blame isn't a practice limited to children. It is a nearly universal, last-ditch attempt on the part of our old Adam to get off the hook and avoid the judgment of the Law.

However, the well-placed "Yeah, but" in a confession is nothing more than self-justification. And that's a problem! Our attempts at self-justification before the Law of God render the true justification offered through the Gospel of Jesus Christ null and void. We can't receive forgiveness if we are still trying to convince God and our own consciences that it really wasn't our fault, that there is really nothing to forgive.

No "Yeah, buts"

What's the answer? Get rid of the buts. Delete the offensive conjunction from our confessions, and teach our students to do the same. Throw ourselves on the mercy of God, without any defense whatsoever, and teach our students to do the same.

Believe the promise that "If we confess our sins, He is faithful and just to forgive us our sins and to cleanse us from all unrighteousness" (1 John 1:9), and through the work of the Holy Spirit, teach our students to do the same.

Things to Think About (or Discuss)

- Right away, I want to start . . .
- Why do I think people use excuses when the Law accuses them?
- What do God's promises offer those who confess their sins? How can I trust that this is so?
- What are three things I can do to teach confession and forgiveness to my students?

26 Developing Christian virtues

Harold L. Senkbeil

An opening thought (to ponder or discuss)

- One thing that bugs me about this new generation of kids is . . .

Read this

One of the signs of a growing spiritual famine in our land is the increasing interest in teaching values to our children. Sensing the deep spiritual vacuum of our time, some concerned parents turn to homeschooling and private education to teach their children right from wrong. They want to give their children a set of positive values they can build their lives around.

As Lutheran teachers, we can only applaud any trend to tackle today's rapidly eroding moral standards. Yet, we can offer our children something far more substantial than mere values.

A word about values and virtues

Values, you see, are notoriously short-lived. They tend to shift and change; they are subjective standards that people choose for themselves.

That's why the older Christian tradition doesn't speak of values at all. Rather, the Church has always focused on teaching *virtues*.

Christian virtues are God's own vision of moral truth, goodness, and faithfulness. These virtues are rooted in the person of Christ Jesus our Lord and are revealed in God's Holy Word. Unlike the more nebulous, undefined concept of personal values, Christian virtues do not depend on human whim and are not validated by human choice.

The value of teaching virtues

When we teach such virtues to our students, we teach the Law of God. And that's crucial, since public morality seems to unravel faster every day.

Note, however, that the Law can only describe; it cannot motivate. That is, we will not make students more godly merely by telling them what God wants them to do or even by threatening them with His punishment.

Rather, they need the life-transforming message of the Gospel of the forgiveness of sins in Jesus' name. In the Gospel alone, Christians are set free from sin and death to live under Christ "in His kingdom and serve Him in everlasting righteousness, innocence, and blessedness" (*Luther's Small Catechism with Explanation*, The Creed, explanation of the Second Article). This new life comes to Christians through the Holy Spirit.

Law and Gospel

So when your lesson covers the clear prohibitions and directives of God's Law, don't shrink from teaching them. We owe it to our children not to be mealymouthed when it comes to teaching Christian virtue: right and wrong according to God's unchanging Word.

But never make the mistake that the Law alone will enable your students to be virtuous. That happens only by the Gospel; make sure each lesson includes a liberal dose. Show your students how Jesus has fulfilled every one of the Father's demands in their place. Show them how He carried all their guilt in His own body on the cross and gives them pardon, comfort, and new minds and hearts through faith in Him.

Things to Think About (or discuss)

- Ah-ha! Now I understand . . .
- Review time. Define God's Law. Describe and define God's Gospel.
- My favorite image for teaching the Gospel is . . . (Some images include slave/free, prisoner/ransom, dead/alive, light/dark, new/old, and lost sheep/Shepherd.)
- List some Christian virtues. (Refresh your list by looking at Ephesians 4:1–7, 17–32.)

27 Teaching how to live as a Christian

John W. Oberdeck

An opening thought (to ponder or discuss)

- Mama always told me that Christians . . .

Read this

How are we to portray the Christian life in our Christian education classes? This simple question unearths more complexity than we might expect, because more is involved here than just our human behavior. How we describe the lives of Christians to our learners can result in genuine confusion of Law and Gospel in their minds, the very thing we want to avoid.

As teachers of the faith, let's review how the Bible describes the lives of Christians and be encouraged to avoid extreme descriptions of the Christian life.

Avoid extremes

Take this sentence, for example: Real Christians don't sin. Though believed by some, this statement is contrary to Lutheran teachings and the Bible. We know that even though we as Christians believe in Jesus Christ as our Lord and Savior, we "daily sin much and surely deserve nothing but punishment," as Luther said in the Small Catechism, in his explanation of the Fifth Petition of the Lord's Prayer.

As long as we are in this life, we fight the devil, the world, and our own sinful flesh. Sometimes we fall. We also know that our status as Christians isn't determined by our behavior—good or bad—but by God's behavior on our behalf through Jesus Christ's death and resurrection, as we have come to trust Jesus by Holy Spirit–given faith.

Nevertheless, our teaching can slip! In subtle ways, we might communicate an expectation of Christian perfection. Perhaps it is in the act of discipline: "Do you really think Christian children behave like that?" Or in describing behaviors to avoid: "Christians don't get drunk!"

These extremes falsely suggest that if we are *truly* Christian, we can evict sin from our lives; and if there still is sin in our lives, we aren't Christians. That's not true!

The old Adam and the new creation

Because of Adam's fall into sin, human beings are born sinners and must struggle with their sinful nature, the old Adam, until they die.

But God does not leave Christians to doubt their faith on account of sin. Rather, by His Spirit, He calls us to repent of our sin, flee to the cross of Jesus, rejoice in the forgiveness of sin, and seek to amend our lives.

"If anyone does sin, we have an advocate with the Father, Jesus Christ the righteous" (1 John 2:1). God sent His Son, Jesus, to pay for our sin. He sends His Holy Spirit through Baptism and the proclamation of the Word to work faith in us and make us a new creation.

Do children and youth in your classes think this deeply over such issues? Probably not. But adults can and do. As we learn more about Law and Gospel in our own lives, we become better equipped to teach our children about the Christian life.

We can help our students recognize the old Adam at work in them when they sin. We can help them rejoice that the new Adam, Jesus Christ, has paid the penalty for their sin and lives in them, making them new by His grace.

Things to Think About (or Discuss)

- Something new I learned about the old and new Adams is . . .
- What part does Baptism play in my understanding of who I am as a Christian?
- What gifts does God give me in Baptism? (For details, see the fourth part of The Sacrament of Holy Baptism in *Luther's Small Catechism with Explanation* and questions 237–260 in the explanation section.)
- How does my identity as a baptized child of God make the way I view life different from the way the world understands it?

28 That's not fair!

David R. Maxwell

AN OPENING THOUGHT (TO PONDER OR DISCUSS)

- A time when I felt treated unfairly was when . . .

Read this

Children are deeply passionate about fairness. If one child gets to stay up late and the other one does not, that's not fair! You can hear the indignation in the protest. Because fairness is easy to relate to, it provides an opportunity to communicate the truths of Law and Gospel.

Like the Law, fairness is good and even necessary in human relationships, but it's not God's last word to us.

Fairness is good

The Bible insists that people treat each other fairly in many ways, including fair weights and measurements (Proverbs 20:23).

Most people, whether Christian or not, agree that fairness is important. At home, parents strive to treat all their children the same. At school, children have a legitimate expectation that their teachers will not show favoritism. When children (and adults) insist on fairness, they are showing that God's Law is written on their hearts (Romans 2:15).

God's Law is holy (Romans 7:12), just as fairness is good. But that does not mean that God's Law (or fairness) is the right approach for every situation. When we start demanding fairness from God, for example, we get into trouble.

Cain was angry that God rejected his sacrifice but accepted his brother Abel's sacrifice. It did not seem fair to him. But God warned Cain that "sin is crouching at the door" (Genesis 4:7) because of that anger. Cain gave in to his anger and ended up killing his brother because of it.

Cain wanted to be treated fairly. We often feel the same way. But think about it! Do we really want the Lord to be fair to us?

Fairness is not God's last word

Fairness means we get what we deserve. However, God's Law shows us that we deserve punishment, even death, because of our sin. Thanks be to God that in Jesus, God does not insist on fairness.

Jesus was innocent, yet He was crucified and the guilty Barabbas was set free (Matthew 27:15–26). That's not fair! More to the point, Jesus suffered punishment for our sins. That's not fair either. Jesus was willing to be treated unfairly for us.

When it comes to our relationship with God, we do not want fairness, and God does not insist on it. God insists on loving us. That might make it a little easier to bear situations where life is not fair.

Things to Think About (or Discuss)

- How did I handle the situation the last time someone told me "It's not fair!"?
- What could I say to children the next time this phrase comes up? to adults?
- How does God's persistent love comfort my students and me when we feel mistreated?

29 Be good!

David R. Maxwell

AN OPENING THOUGHT (TO PONDER OR DISCUSS)

- Something I am good at is . . .

Read this

Children are used to being told to "be good." Parents and teachers urge this ideal on children all the time. A good child is one who pays attention and does not disrupt the class. A bad child cuts up and perhaps even rebels against the teacher.

This notion of good and bad is common sense, and it would be impossible to run a class without any distinction between good and bad behavior.

The Law condemns bad behavior

At the same time, we confess that we are "by nature sinful and unclean." When asked to describe our spiritual condition, Lutherans are accustomed to admitting that we are sinners.

Not all denominations or Christian publishers admit this, and some do not teach about our sinfulness in their curriculum. For example, lessons might ignore the topic of sin and our need for a Savior; or they might only define sin as outward behavior, not as a sinful and fatal condition. This is a fatal flaw because it affects how Christians understand (1) who we are without Christ, and (2) the magnitude of the gift God gives us through the sacrificial death and resurrection of Jesus.

For Lutherans, the idea that we could actually claim to be good goes against every fiber of our being. This shows that the Law is doing its job. The Law accuses us and prevents us from relying on our works for salvation.

Yet we have no problem making a distinction between "good" and "bad" when it comes to children's behavior in the classroom. Why is that?

The Law praises good behavior

We might expect to hear that the Gospel is somehow the answer, but in this case, that is not so. When we speak of good and bad behavior in the classroom, we are not saying that the Gospel blesses good behavior and condemns bad behavior.

The notion that good behavior should be praised is actually Law, not Gospel. So we find ourselves in a position where we say that we cannot keep the Law, and then we turn around and urge our children to be "good." Is that a contradiction? It is not, as long as you understand what sphere the Law is operating in.

When it comes to our relationship to God, the Law can only condemn us; it cannot win God's favor. However, when it comes to relationships with other people, as in classroom management, the Law can and does provide order. It rewards as well as punishes.

The Gospel gives identity

Yet, the Gospel has something to do with classroom behavior too. The Gospel gives students their identity—not determined by good or bad behavior, but by the fact that they (and we) are God's children through Baptism. As God's children, we possess the dignity and honor of Christ Himself, since we are clothed with Christ (Galatians 3:27). This fact shapes how everyone in the class views and behaves toward one another.

Things to Think About [or discuss]

- How does a statement like "Christians don't act that way" define children as good or bad?
- How does calling children good or bad affect their understanding of who they are and what they need from Jesus?
- How does knowing classmates are God's children through Baptism change the way students view each other?
- What benefits do I see in curriculum that teaches Law and Gospel? that emphasizes Baptism and students' identity as children of God? that teaches about the gifts God gives us through Christ's body and blood in the Lord's Supper? Why might publishers leave out these points?
- Does the current curriculum teach Law and Gospel? Does it emphasize Baptism? Does it teach a right understanding of the Lord's Supper? If not, what can I do?

30 Using rewards and punishments

John W. Oberdeck

An opening thought (to ponder or discuss)

- My favorite reward to give myself is . . .

Read this

Imagine: Your son has developed discipline problems at home, and you are determined to improve his behavior. You know that rewards and punishments are useful in changing behavior, so you praise your son's positive actions and punish his poor choices. Sharing with his sister brings him a candy bar. Locking his sister in the closet brings an extended time-out. He notices what's happening, and his behavior begins to improve. Wonderful!

But in the back of your mind you wonder, "Am I really doing the right thing? Am I somehow messing up the faith life of my child? Won't he inevitably begin to think he is saved by his good deeds? Won't he develop a 'works righteousness' attitude toward life?"

Law or Gospel?

Great questions! You know intuitively that these questions are about Law and Gospel. You know that the Law is not a pathway to salvation. You know the Gospel is a completely free gift from God, forgiveness of sins through faith in the life, death, and resurrection of Jesus Christ. You sense that behavior modification techniques are a Law-oriented approach. What do you do?

Before you abandon rewards and punishments, here are two things to keep in mind.

First, using rewards and punishments will not train your child to seek righteousness through works. Your child already knows that path. In fact, we all by nature and from birth seek righteousness through works of the Law. In theological terms this is called the *opinio legis,* the belief that God's grace and favor are gained through human works. The fallen human nature naturally thinks this way.

In faith, you realize the *opinio legis* is wrong; God saves you. You do not save yourself. We fight against the *opinio legis* by daily drowning the old Adam through our Baptism and rising as a new creation in Jesus Christ. This means we daily confess our sins to God and remember that in our Baptism, He forgives and makes us His much-loved children. This daily action reinforces our identity, sets us free from sin, and empowers us to serve the Lord gladly!

Second, there is nothing wrong with you or your child or your Christian education class anticipating rewards. Deeds done in faith, as God's baptized children, give glory to God. For the sake of Christ, God sees us washed clean of sin and sinful motivation for works.

Good deeds are good only because Jesus makes them good through His perfect life, atoning suffering and death, and victorious resurrection. They are done in faith and give glory to God. They are not done according to the Law to bring salvation.

So back to rewarding your child or your class. Can you do it? I believe you can.

First, share that the Holy Spirit enables us, in faith, to do good things. Second, emphasize that good deeds are good because Jesus makes them good. Third, affirm their good behavior and emphasize that because of our faith in Christ, God is pleased when His children honor Him with their behavior. Then celebrate what was done with the reward of your choice.

Things to Think About (or Discuss)

- List the three things the reading said to do to teach children about good behavior.
- What's my favorite way to reward children? adults?
- How can I daily drown the old Adam through Baptism? What benefits are received from this action? (For help, see the fourth part of The Sacrament of Baptism and questions 255–56 and 259 in *Luther's Small Catechism with Explanation*.)
- When and how can I find time for daily confession and drowning of the old Adam?

31 Don't be mean!

John W. Oberdeck

An opening thought (to ponder or discuss)

- A behavior that I think is just plain mean is . . .

Read this

"Mean-spirited Christian!" That's the last label you want, isn't it?

Followers of Jesus, to the best of their ability in a fallen world, imitate their Lord and Savior by acts of service and love. Believers are kind, tenderhearted, and forgiving. Blessed by the love of Jesus, believers seek to always trust, always hope, and always persevere (1 Corinthians 13:7). Believers are nice, especially Christian education teachers!

The Law hurts

But think again. God's Law, when spoken clearly, offends the sinner's ear. God's Law exposes not only gross and obvious sins worthy of condemnation; God's Law also prosecutes the minor infractions with the same wrath and eternal punishment! No one is exempt from the Law's accusations. When the Law is heard correctly, it hurts. No wonder people hearing the Law may respond defensively! "Those mean-spirited Christians. They are so judgmental! They are such hypocrites!"

Now, we don't want to be mean-spirited, judgmental, or hypocritical, do we? To avoid the poor public-relations possibilities, we might avoid teaching the Law, hoping that people inside and outside the Church find our message more appealing—or at the very least, less offensive.

Why is this a mistake? For two reasons: first, because speaking the Law is not mean-spirited, and second, because not speaking the Law is mean-spirited.

The Law is not mean

Speaking the Law is no more mean-spirited than trying to warn a driver speeding toward a road-construction site that the bridge is out. Though the Law warns us of God's wrath and punishment, God is not mean-spirited in giving the Law. Quite the contrary!

By revealing to us in the Scriptures what we, as His creatures, must be like in order to please Him, God defines for us what sin has done to our relationship with Him. The Law wakes us up to the reality that we are, by nature, spiritually blind, dead, and enemies of God. The Law drives us to Christ. By using the Law in this way, God leads us to the cross of Jesus Christ. He prepares us to hear the Gospel.

If we don't teach God's Law, then we really are mean-spirited and judgmental. What could be more callous than denying people the truth? Without an understanding of Law, people think Jesus is nothing more than a good example. With an understanding of Law, people are led to hear the Good News that Jesus is their only Savior from sin.

We teach using Law and Gospel, therefore, knowing that in sharing the whole counsel of God, we aren't mean-spirited, but kind-spirited Christians.

Things to Think About (or discuss)

- How is it mean *not* to teach the Law?
- Practice words to say if someone says Christians are hypocrites.
- What happens when I realize I am spiritually blind, dead, and an enemy of God?
- What comfort does the Gospel offer when others have harmed me? (For more insights, read Romans 12:14–21.)

32 Are you mad at me?

Bryan Wolfmueller

AN OPENING THOUGHT (TO PONDER OR DISCUSS)

- Share a recent "uh-oh" moment.

Read this

Crash! Maybe it was a lamp, a plate, a picture in a frame, but now it is a bunch of pieces on the floor. We all remember being the child who just broke something, standing over a piece of our own destruction, hearing Mom's footsteps getting closer. We all remember the shock and the fear. And I suspect that we all remember looking up at Mom's face as tears begin to form, asking, "Are you mad at me?"

That's a good question

"Are you mad at me?" This is the most important question children have for their parents.

And it's an important question for us Christians, the children of God, to ask our Father. "God, are You mad at me?" We know that God should be angry. We know we've done much worse than break a lamp. We've sinned against God, despised His Word, spurned His love, been indifferent to His gifts. We've been lazy, selfish, self-serving, and proud. We've ignored our neighbors' needs and even caused them harm. We have sinned, and this sin calls forth God's wrath, His anger. God should be mad at us.

But the Good News of the Gospel is that our heavenly Father is not mad at us. He poured out all His wrath and anger on His Son, Jesus, on the cross. His anger toward us is spent, used up.

This is the wonderful and comforting promise Isaiah gives: "I will give thanks to You, O LORD, for though You were angry with me, Your anger turned away, that You might comfort me" (Isaiah 12:1).

God's anger has been deflected, turned away by the cross and the blood of Jesus. Give thanks to God; He is not mad at us! In the wonderful mystery of Law and Gospel, we don't get what we deserve. The Gospel turns away God's wrath and brings instead His love, mercy, and forgiveness.

All of us know what it's like to be in trouble. We know the terrible feeling of someone being mad at us. When we ask God, "Are You mad at me?" the marvelous answer comes back, "No, absolutely not. I love you." This is blessed news indeed—for us, for our students, and for all of the Lord's dear children.

THINGS TO THINK ABOUT [OR DISCUSS]

- Name a Bible story that tells about God's wrath.
- How do I feel when someone should be mad at me but isn't?
- How does the child-Father imagery help or hinder my understanding of God's love for me? How could I improve my thinking about this?
- How does God comfort me?

33 Blessing those you teach

Roger Sonnenberg

An opening thought (to ponder or discuss)

- Something I looked for in all the wrong places is . . .

Read this

Do you know anyone who is an extreme perfectionist, a workaholic? That person is driven to be accepted, to be loved. Or have you known people who desire recognition so much that they seek love and acceptance in all the wrong places?

The Blessing, a book by Gary Smalley and John Trent, looks at what drives such people. These people may never have felt blessed. They feel they've never done enough or been good enough to meet the expectations of others. They live under the Law. They have missed the blessing. They cry out with Esau, "Bless me, even me also, O my father!" (Genesis 27:34).

Unconditional love

Human beings have a universal need for unconditional love. Yet, in every Christian education setting, there are people who feel unloved or see love as something they need to earn or deserve. Since the fall, our sinful nature has affected every person in the same way.

As hard as we try to be good enough to deserve love, eventually we must conclude with the apostle Paul that we are not very lovable: "I do not understand my own actions. For I do not do what I want, but I do the very thing I hate. . . . Who will deliver me from this body of death?" (Romans 7:15, 24).

What a privilege it is, then, to share the truth about God's unconditional love for His people! We can talk and sing about a God who gave up His only-begotten Son to redeem us, to bring us back into a loving relationship with Him. We can celebrate the Gospel—the Good News that we are freed from the guilt, the punishment, and the power of sin and are loved!

Scriptural blessing

In studying the Old and New Testament blessings, Trent and Smalley discovered that there were five key elements attached to most blessings in Scripture: (1) meaningful touch; (2) a spoken message; (3) a high value attached to the one being blessed; (4) a special future envisioned for the one being blessed; and (5) an active commitment to fulfill the blessing.

Each element contributes to blessing another person. Each helps the receiver know that he or she is loved. As teachers, pastors, DCEs, and lay leaders, we can offer such blessings to those we teach.

Does our teaching suggest that our students must earn our love and God's? Instead, by the things we say and do, let's share a Gospel blessing, telling students that they have a God who loves them "without any merit or worthiness" on their part. Yes, there's always a place for the teaching of the Law, but over and above everything, there must be the sharing of the Gospel!

Things to Think About (or Discuss)

- How can singing hymns and spiritual songs bless my students and me?
- How could I share a group blessing with my students each week?
- How could I share an individual blessing with every student at every class? (For example, touch each person's shoulder as they leave and say a brief encouraging word, such as "May God give you courage to live as His child" or "God keep you in His grace this week.")
- How could taking time for individual blessings change my relationships with my students?

34 The last[ing] Word

Carl Fickenscher II

An opening thought [to ponder or discuss]

A few things that have lasted or endured in my life are . . .

Read this

Why is it that all too many parents, even active members, send their children to Christian education but don't attend themselves? Maybe it's because they forget Christian education is about eternal things. They focus on its effects in time rather than in eternity.

In time

You've probably heard comments like these:

> "Sunday School? Oh, yeah, it's important for kids to learn right from wrong and respect for authority so they don't do drugs or have sex before marriage."
>
> "Me? I went. I'm glad I did. It kept me out of trouble."
>
> "She's the right age, so she has to go to confirmation. It's our family tradition, and it'll help her to know a little about God."

These comments reflect a common but mistaken application of God's Word.

C. F. W. Walther addressed this problem when he said, "You are not rightly distinguishing Law and Gospel in the Word of God if you use the demands, threats, or promises of the Law to try and force the unregenerate to put away their sins and engage in good works and thus become godly" or if the person teaching it does "not allow the Gospel to predominate in your teaching" (*Law and Gospel: How to Read and Apply the Bible*, Theses XXIII and XXV).

It's true that Christian education does foster wholesome observance of God's commands, but obedience motivated by the Law has value only in our present life and perhaps for only a short time.

The Law—what God requires us to do or not do—can indeed move one to outward good by threats or rewards. But anything done to avoid punishment or gain a reward is ultimately selfish, not done for God or neighbor but for oneself. Such works do not please God and will pass away, to be long forgotten in eternity.

In eternity

Christian education is about eternal things—even when it comes to good works. It is, as Walther said, predominantly about the Gospel. Everything in Christian education, including the Law, points to what God has done for us in Christ Jesus. Christ became one of us, died on the cross, and rose from the grave to give us eternal life. The same Gospel of Christ Jesus is the one and only motivation God uses to establish our works as lasting, eternal.

When we realize—by the promise of the Gospel—that we have everything we could ever dream of and more—for all eternity—then the believer in us does works that are truly good and from a selfless motive, because we know there's nothing further we could gain for ourselves. Those works, God says, have eternal value.

Of course, the very same Gospel of Christ Jesus is the reminder the Holy Spirit uses to keep us in faith, to keep us possessing our eternal blessing. It is the Word we need constantly throughout our lives, every day. And it is the Word that should predominate every week in Christian education classes—the Word of the Gospel.

Things to Think About (or Discuss)

- Why does obedience motivated by the Law have value only in the present life? Why is Law-motivated obedience short-term?
- What works have eternal value?
- How is Christianity about eternal things?
- What can I do to help parents see that Christian education is about important, eternal things?

Appendix

C. F. W. Walther's Law and Gospel Theses

Thesis 1: The doctrinal contents of all Holy Scripture, both of the Old and the New Testament, consist of two doctrines that differ fundamentally from each other. These two doctrines are Law and Gospel.

Thesis 2: If you wish to be an orthodox teacher, you must present all the articles of faith in accordance with Scripture, yet [you] must also rightly **distinguish** Law and Gospel.

Thesis 3: To rightly distinguish Law and Gospel is the most difficult and highest Christian art—and for theologians in particular. It is taught only by the Holy Spirit in combination with experience.

Thesis 4: Understanding how to distinguish Law and Gospel provides **wonderful insight** for understanding all of Holy Scripture correctly. In fact, without this knowledge Scripture is and remains a sealed book.

Thesis 5: The most common way people mingle Law and Gospel—and one that is also the easiest to detect because it is so crude—is prevalent among Papists, Socinians, and Rationalists. These people turn Christ into a kind of new Moses or Lawgiver. This transforms the Gospel into a doctrine of meritorious works. Furthermore, some people—like the Papists—condemn and anathematize those who teach that the Gospel is the message of the free grace of God in Christ.

Thesis 6: You are not rightly distinguishing Law and Gospel in the Word of God if you do not preach the Law in its full sternness and the Gospel in its full sweetness. Similarly, do not mingle Gospel elements with the Law or Law elements with the Gospel.

Thesis 7: You are not rightly distinguishing Law and Gospel in the Word of God if you first preach the Gospel and then the Law, or first sanctification and then justification, or first faith and then repentance, or first good works and then grace.

Thesis 8: You are not rightly distinguishing Law and Gospel in the Word of God if you preach the Law to those who are already in terror on account of their sins or the Gospel to those who are living securely in their sins.

Thesis 9: You are not rightly distinguishing Law and Gospel in the Word of God if you point sinners who have been struck down and terrified by the Law toward their own prayers and struggles with God and tell them that they have to work their way into a state of grace. That is, do not tell them to keep on praying and struggling until they would feel that God has received them into grace. Rather, point them toward the Word and Sacraments.

Thesis 10: You are not rightly distinguishing Law and Gospel in the Word of God if you preach that "dead" faith can justify and save in the sight of God—while that believer is still living in mortal sins. In the same way, do not preach that faith justifies and saves those unrepentant people because of the love and renewal it produces in them.

Thesis 11: You are not rightly distinguishing Law and Gospel in the Word of God if you only want to comfort those with the Gospel who are contrite because they love God. You also need to comfort people with the Gospel who are only contrite because they fear His wrath and punishment.

Thesis 12: You are not rightly distinguishing Law and Gospel in the Word of God if you teach that the reason our sins are forgiven is because we both believe and are contrite.

Thesis 13: You are not rightly distinguishing Law and Gospel in the Word of God if you explain faith by demanding that people are able to make themselves believe or at least can collaborate toward that end. Rather, preach faith into people's hearts by laying the Gospel promises before them.

Thesis 14: You are not rightly distinguishing Law and Gospel in the Word of God if you demand that faith is a condition for justification and salvation. It would be wrong to preach that people are righteous in the sight of God and are saved not only *by* their faith, but also *on account of* their faith, *for the sake of* their faith, or *in view of* their faith.

Thesis 15: You are not rightly distinguishing Law and Gospel in the Word of God if you turn the Gospel into a preaching of repentance.

Thesis 16: You are not rightly distinguishing Law and Gospel in the Word of God if you claim that people are truly converted when they get rid of certain vices and, instead, engage in certain works of piety and virtuous practices.

Thesis 17: You are not rightly distinguishing Law and Gospel in the Word of God if you describe believers in a way that is not always realistic—both with regard to the strength of their faith and to the feeling and fruitfulness of their faith.

Thesis 18: You are not rightly distinguishing Law and Gospel in the Word of God if you describe the universal corruption of mankind so as to create the impression that even true believers are still under the spell of ruling sins and sin deliberately.

Thesis 19: You are not rightly distinguishing Law and Gospel in the Word of God if you preach about certain sins as if they were not damnable but only venial.

Thesis 20: You are not rightly distinguishing Law and Gospel in the Word of God if a person's salvation is made to depend on his association with the visible orthodox Church and if you claim that salvation is denied to every person erring in any article of faith.

Thesis 21: You are not rightly distinguishing Law and Gospel in the Word of God if you teach that the Sacraments save *ex opere operato,* that is, merely by their outward performance.

Thesis 22: You are not rightly distinguishing Law and Gospel in the Word of God if a false distinction is made between a person's being awakened and being converted; moreover, when a person's **inability** to believe is mistaken for not being **permitted** to believe.

Thesis 23: You are not rightly distinguishing Law and Gospel in the Word of God if you use the demands, threats, or promises of the Law to try and force the unregenerate to put away their sins and engage in good works and thus become godly; and then, on the other hand, if you use the commands of the Law—rather than the admonitions of the Gospel—to urge the regenerate to do good.

Thesis 24: You are not rightly distinguishing Law and Gospel in the Word of God if you claim the unforgivable sin against the Holy Spirit cannot be forgiven because of its magnitude.

Thesis 25: You are not rightly distinguishing Law and Gospel in the Word of God if you do not allow the Gospel to predominate in your teaching.